A Family in Italy

A pronunciation guide for the Italian words and
names used in this book appears on page 28.

LIBRARY OF CONGRESS CATALOGING-IN-PUBLICATION DATA

Hubley, Penny.
    A family in Italy.

    Rev. ed. of: Italian family. © 1986.
    Summary: Describes the home, school, amusements,
customs, and work of an eight-year-old girl and her
family living in a small town outside of Florence.
    1. Italy—Social life and customs—Juvenile
literature. 2. Florence Region (Italy)—Social life
and customs—Juvenile literature. [1. Italy—Social
life and customs. 2. Family life—Italy] I. Hubley,
John. II. Hubley, Penny. Italian family. III. Title.
DG451.H83 1987   945′.51   86-27228
ISBN 0-8225-1673-X (lib. bdg.)

Manufactured in the United States of America

    2   3   4   5   6   7   8   9   10   96   95   94   93   92   91   90   89

A Family in Italy

Penny and John Hubley

Lerner Publications Company • Minneapolis

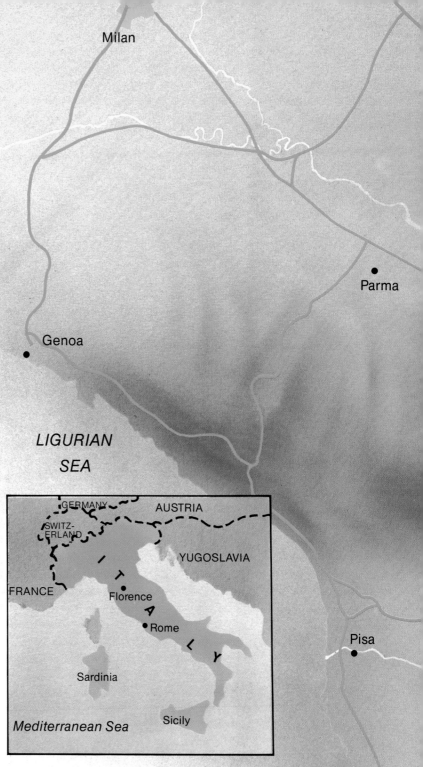

Milan

Parma

Genoa

LIGURIAN
SEA

This is Francesca Rossi. She's eight years old and lives in Grassina in northern Italy. Grassina is a small town about six miles (10 kilometers) from Florence. It's a very old town and its name comes from a Roman family who once lived there.

GERMANY   AUSTRIA

SWITZ-
ERLAND

YUGOSLAVIA

I
T
A

FRANCE

Florence

Rome

L
Y

Sardinia

Pisa

Sicily

Mediterranean Sea

4

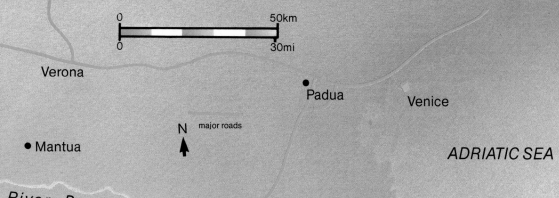

major roads

Verona

Padua

Venice

ADRIATIC SEA

Mantua

N

River Po

Ferrara

Modena

Bologna

Florence

Grassina

Greve

Francesca has lived in Grassina only three years. Before that, her family lived in the country near a town called Greve. They moved so that Francesca's father could be nearer to his work. Francesca's grandparents still live in Greve, and she often goes to see them. It only takes thirty minutes by car, but it's a twisty mountain road and it seems like a long trip.

Francesca and her parents live in a new apartment building, on the second floor. Francesca likes the apartment because it was built especially for her family.

When the family decided to move to Grassina, they joined a group of people called a cooperative. Some people in the cooperative were friends and some had seen it advertised in the newspapers. The group all worked together to borrow the money from a bank and hire the architects and builders. When the building was finished, everyone moved in.

Behind the apartment building there's a park that everybody shares. The park was the last thing to be finished. Francesca's family and their neighbors had a huge party to celebrate and everyone brought food. Francesca's father brought some ham and carved a piece for everyone.

They wanted to have the party in the park, but it was pouring with rain, so they had to hold the party under cover by the parking lot. It was such a good party that nobody minded.

Every morning at 8:00 A.M., Francesca catches a school bus with her friends. Her school is on the other side of town. It's called Scuola Elementaria Marconi, named after a famous Italian inventor.

On weekdays, Francesca is at school from 8:30 until 4:30. There's school on Saturday mornings, too. Most grade schools have shorter hours but Francesca's mother and father send her to this one because they have to work all day.

Because the day is so long, the class has two different teachers. There's one for the mornings and another for the afternoons. Nearly everybody in the class likes the morning teacher because she often brings her guitar along and they all join in singing. Francesca's favorite song is hard to sing, because the words are in French, Russian, and English as well as Italian.

Francesca's in the second grade with 25 other children in her class. She's best at writing stories and drawing pictures. She doesn't like gym class at all.

Francesca stays at school for lunch. There isn't a school dining room, so they clear all the books away, put down tablecloths, and eat at their desks. The food is cooked in the school kitchen and the students take turns serving. Today they're having chicken, which is Francesca's favorite.

During the day there are long recesses when everyone goes out onto the school playground. The boys all play soccer, which is called *calcio* in Italy. Grassina has two amateur clubs but most of the boys are fans of Fiorentina, which is Florence's professional team.

Francesca's father used to play soccer when he was a boy. Now he's a volleyball fan. His favorite team is the Grassina team, and sometimes he takes Francesca to the league games. Home matches are played at the Casa di Popolo. That is the working-men's club, which is used as the town's community center. The Grassina team won the national championship there last year.

At the end of June, school ends for three months. During the summer vacation, Francesca sometimes takes the bus to Florence for the day to visit her cousins. Before the bus arrives, she has to buy her ticket from a coffee shop.

In Florence there are always thousands of tourists. They fill all the bars and street cafes. Most of them come to see the famous buildings and paintings. The city gets so crowded in the summer that the tourists stay in hotels as far away as Grassina.

Florence is a very old city. It was founded by soldiers from Julius Caesar's army. Its modern name in Italian is Firenze. Near the city you can see buildings that the Romans left, like the Roman theatre in the picture on the right.

In the past, the cities of Italy each had their own rulers. When Italy became one nation, Florence was the capital city for five years. Rome became the capital in 1870.

The first two weeks of August are a national holiday in Italy and all the factories and stores close. It's called Feragosto, which means August Fair. Most years the Rossis go away to the sea on the west coast of Italy.

Francesca's father, Alberto, works in a factory in the north of Florence. There aren't any large factories in Grassina, so a lot of people commute to work in the city. Signor Rossi drives there every day in his new car. It's an Italian Fiat and he's very proud of it. Every weekend he spends time polishing it and tinkering with the engine.

Signor Rossi's job is making molds for plastic bottles. He makes the molds from strong metal and then neatens any rough edges, using special drills. It is a very skilled job and it took him years to learn.

When the molds are ready, they are sent to other factories where the bottles are made. Hot plastic is blown into a mold. As the plastic cools, it hardens into a bottle shape. The mold is taken off and the bottle is finished. Lots of things are sold in the bottles made from Signor Rossi's molds.

The factory where Francesca's father works is small, but the molds he makes are sent to places all over the world, including Britain, North America, and the Middle East.

Francesca's mother, Renata, works at home as a dressmaker. A company delivers the cloth to the apartment, cut and ready to sew. Signora Rossi and her neighbors divide the work between them.

Because she likes fresh food, Signora Rossi goes shopping nearly every day. She can get everything she needs from the shops in Grassina.

The first thing on her list is a joint of lamb, which she gets from the butcher's.

Then Signora Rossi goes on to the fish dealer's van to buy some clams. She'll cook them in a sauce to eat with spaghetti.

Next, Signora Rossi gets about a pound (half a kilo) of the local farm-house cheese and some ham.

On Fridays, there's an open-air market in the town square. Signora Rossi buys her fruit and vegetables from a booth there because they're usually fresh.

Francesca's father loves salami, so her mother picks out a couple of good ones for him. Signora Rossi also gets a magazine for Francesca that says what's on each of the nine channels of TV each week.

The last thing on Signora Rossi's list is pasta. The family starts most evening meals with pasta with a sauce on top. Then they have meat and vegetables, and fresh fruit to follow.

Francesca's mother usually buys dried pasta from the supermarket. It isn't as good as the fresh pasta, but it's much cheaper. She only buys fresh pasta for special occasions.

Signor Rossi has a friend who runs a small business making pasta. The pasta comes in all sorts of shapes and sizes. The most popular kind is spaghetti. The machine in the picture is making *tortellini*. These are little pasta pockets stuffed with a meat filling.

Pasta is made from wheat flour mixed with oil, water, and salt. The dough is flattened into a huge sheet. Then the machine cuts out pieces of dough. To make tortellini, it cuts out circles and wraps each around a little bit of filling. A fan blows air onto the pasta to keep it from sticking to the machine.

On her way home, Signora Rossi stops for a cup of coffee at the Bar Sergio. She usually drinks her coffee standing inside at the counter. In summer, people can sit at the tables on the sidewalk outside. Signora Rossi doesn't often do this because if you sit down, you have to pay more.

The coffee shop sells all kinds of fresh cakes, pastries, and cookies. Mario, the pastry cook, is an old friend of the Rossi family. He has to start work at four o'clock in the morning so the pastries are ready when the shop opens at seven.

Francesca's favorite cookies are the ones with jam on top. When she goes to the shop with her mother, Mario always puts an extra cookie in the bag as a treat for her. Francesca loves to stop there, even if Mario does tease her.

The shop is open every day except Tuesday, and it doesn't shut until nine in the evening. People use it as a meeting place to stop and talk. There are eight coffee shops in Grassina, and each one has its regular customers who go to have coffee and a snack before work.

On weekends, Francesca's parents often take her to visit her grandparents. They live in an old farmhouse in Greve, which is about twelve miles (19 kilometers) from Grassina.

Francesca thinks it would be nice to live in the country, but her father says it's hard work living on a farm.

Francesca's grandfather grows peaches, apricots, olives, and grapes. He trades most of these with his neighbors for other things, such as meat and cheese, or for the loan of farm equipment. Anything that's left over is sold in the local market.

Grandfather Rossi's pride is his garden. In it he grows vegetables for the family. He's especially proud of his artichokes, tomatoes, and lettuce, and waters them carefully through the long, dry summer.

Spring is a busy time for Francesca's grandfather. If he doesn't cut back the olive trees, they grow spindly and don't produce many olives. Although he is an old man, he climbs the ladder and prunes them himself. He says that some of the trees are a hundred years old and still producing olives.

Francesca's grandfather doesn't keep animals any more because he finds it difficult to manage the farm on his own. He understands why his sons took jobs in the city, but he's sad that there is no one else to take over the farm.

On the farm, Grandfather Rossi grows grapes. He makes his own wine for the family to drink with their meals. The farm is in the Chianti region of Italy, which is famous for red wine.

Nearby there is an ancient castle which once belonged to an early explorer of America, Giovanni da Verrazzano. A statue of him stands in the Greve market square. His family still lives in the castle and makes wine.

In the spring, the grapevines are cut back and tied to supports with willow twigs to make sure that they grow up straight.

The grapes start to grow in the summer and by October they are ripe and ready to be picked. The juice is squeezed out of the grapes in a huge press. Then it is kept in large oak barrels to ferment into wine.

When the wine is ready to drink, it is put into bottles. On the labels there is a picture of Giovanni da Verrazzano. Most of the wine is sent out to the United States and to other countries in Europe, but some even goes to Australia.

Francesca's grandparents are busy in the spring, but they always find time to invite the family over for Easter dinner. Francesca tells them how excited she is about the raffle tickets she has bought. Every shop has an Easter raffle and Francesca thinks she might be lucky and win a giant chocolate egg.

Although many people in Italy are devout Catholics, the Rossi family doesn't go to church. They do join in some of the Easter celebrations, and everyone helps to prepare dinner on Easter Sunday.

Grandfather Rossi opens a bottle of wine, Francesca's mother cooks the pasta, and Signor Rossi carves the chicken. Then they end their meal with a special, traditional, cross-shaped cake. Francesca gets to cut the first slice.

Italian Words in This Book

Francesca Rossi fran-CHESS-kah ROSS-ee
Grassina GRASS-ee-nah
Greve GREH-veh
Scuola Elementaria Marconi skoo-OH-lah
  ell-em-en-TA-ree-ah MAR-coh-nee
calcio KAHL-cho
Fiorentina fyor-en-TEE-nah
Casa di Popolo KAH-zah dee POH-poh-loh
Firenze fih-RENZ-eh
Feragosto fair-ah-GOS-toh
Alberto al-BER-toh
Signor see-NYOR
Renata ree-NAH-tah
Signora see-NYOH-rah
tortellini tor-tel-LEE-nee
Bar Sergio BAHR SER-gee-oh
Mario MA-ree-oh
Chianti kee-AHN-tee
Giovanni da Verrazzano gee-oh-VAH-nee
  dah ver-at-ZAH-noh

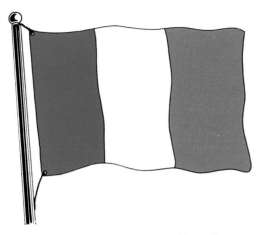

Facts about Italy

Official Name: Italian Republic

Capital: Rome

Official Language: Italian
There are many different dialects of Italian spoken in the different regions of Italy. Standard Italian is based on the Tuscan dialect.

Form of Money: lira

Area: 116,314 square miles (302,252 square kilometers)
Italy is about as large as the state of Arizona.

Population: over 56 million people
The United States has about four times as many people as Italy.

NORTH
AMERICA

SOUTH
AMERICA

EUROPE

ASIA

Italy

AFRICA

AUSTRALIA

31

Families the World Over

Some children in foreign countries live like you do. Others live very differently. In these books, you can meet children from all over the world. You'll learn about their games and schools, their families and friends, and what it's like to grow up in a faraway land.

Lerner Publications Company, 241 First Avenue North, Minneapolis, Minnesota 55401